**GIRL TALK**

# LOOKING GOOD

## Style Secrets for Girls

### STEPHANIE TURNBULL

**A+**
**Smart Apple Media**

Published by Smart Apple Media, an imprint of Black Rabbit Books
P.O. Box 3263, Mankato, Minnesota 56002
www.blackrabbitbooks.com

Library of Congress Cataloging-in-Publication Data

Turnbull, Stephanie.
Looking good : style secrets for girls / by Stephanie Turnbull.
pages cm.—(Girl talk)
Summary: "Perfect for girls that are interested in the style secrets for looking
and feeling their best. Topics include body basics, hair care, finding a unique style,
thinking positive, and feeling happy. This book gives the advice and inspiration for girls to
look and feel fantastic"-- Provided by publisher.
Audience: Grade 4 to 6.
Includes bibliographical references and index.
ISBN 978-1-59920-948-7 (library binding : alk. paper)
1. Teenage girls—Health and hygiene. 2. Beauty, Personal. 3. Grooming for girls. I. Title.
RA777.25.T87 2014
646.7'042—dc23
                    2012039794

Created by Appleseed Editions Ltd,
Designed and illustrated by Guy Callaby
Edited by Mary-Jane Wilkins

Picture credits
t = top, b = bottom, l = left, r = right, c = center
page 1 Ingram Publishing/Thinkstock; 2t Hemera/Thinkstock, b iStockphoto/Thinkstock; 3 Maxim Godkin/
Shutterstock; 4l Jupiterimages/Thinkstock, r Brad Sauter/Shutterstock; 5l Losevsky Photo and Video/Shutterstock.
com, b Hemera/Thinkstock, r Victorian Traditions/Shutterstock.com; 6r Odua Images/Shutterstock, l Aaron
Amat/Shutterstock; 7tl Evgeny Karandaev/Shutterstock, tr DenisNata/Shutterstock, c Shmel/Shutterstock,
b adam36/Shutterstock; 8t BestPhotoPlus/Shutterstock, b fotofreaks/Shutterstock; 9t Nikola Bilic/Shutterstock,
bl iStockphoto/Thinkstock, br michaeljung/Shutterstock; 10 iStockphoto/Thinkstock, r iStockphoto/Thinkstock,
b travis manley/Shutterstock; 11 CREATISTA/Shutterstock; 12 samotrebizan/Shutterstock; 12l Michelle D.
Milliman/Shutterstock; 13t Maugli/Shutterstock, b Everett Collection/Shutterstock; 14t DenisNata/Shutterstock,
l Julija Sapic/Shutterstock, b James Clarke/Shutterstock; 15tl Hemera/Thinkstock, tr NatUlrich/Shutterstock,
r xymmus/Shutterstock, b HamsterMan/Shutterstock; 16 Digital Vision/Thinkstock; 17 new vave/Shutterstock,
r iStockphoto/Thinkstock; 18l samotrebizan/Shutterstock, r Garsya/Shutterstock; 19t BaLL LunLa/Shutterstock,
b Elena Elisseeva/Shutterstock; 20t Africa Studio/Shutterstock, l akiyoko/Shutterstock; 21t (buttons) iStockphoto/
Thinkstock, Georgios Kollidas/Shutterstock, bl feiyuwzhangjie/shutterstock.com, br catwalker/shutterstock.com;
22t, r, l, b all iStockphoto/Thinkstock; 23l Hemera Technologies/Thinkstock, r iStockphoto/Thinkstock;
24l panpote/Shutterstock, Comstock Images/Thinkstock, tr kedrov/Shutterstock, cr Guzel/Shutterstock,
br winnond/Shutterstock; 25l Vitaly Titov & Maria Sidelnikova/Shutterstock, r Graça Victoria/Shutterstock,
c SeDmi/Shutterstock, b cenap refik ongan/Shutterstock; 26 Marilyn Volan/Shutterstock; 27t
iStockphoto/Thinkstock, r David Davis/Shutterstock, b iStockphoto/Thinkstock; 28 Elena Elisseeva/
Shutterstock;
29t Tracy Whiteside/Shutterstock, b Jaren Jai Wicklund/Shutterstock, r Lena Sergeeva/Shutterstock;
30 iStockhoto; 31 iStockphoto; 32 lev dolgachov/Shutterstock
Front cover iStockphoto/Thinkstock

Printed in the United States at Corporate Graphics in North Mankato, Minnesota.
PO DAD5005a
102013

9 8 7 6 5 4 3 2

# Contents

# Style Secrets

**L**ooking good means so much more than just dressing well. It's about taking care of your body, following your own style, thinking positive, and feeling happy. This book gives you all the advice and inspiration you need to look and feel fantastic—without spending a fortune!

You and your friends may each have quite different style ideas.

## The Real You

The key to looking great is to make the most of what you already have. Don't try to give yourself a complete image makeover. It won't last and you'll feel like a fake. Instead, think carefully about what suits you and makes you feel comfortable.

## Think Smart!

Use your head when it comes to beauty and fashion. Just because a magazine or an ad says something is fashionable, it doesn't always mean it's right for you. And remember that advertisers want you to spend more and more money. Which is why magazines have a new "must-have" look every week.

If a magazine said this looked good, would you wear it?

### Pssst... Hot Tip!

Look out for these tips throughout the book. They give you all kinds of extra style ideas, tricks, and help.

## Want to Wear This?

Rich girls in the 1600s wore fussy silk dresses, while poorer girls had thick, scratchy woolen frocks.

In the 1840s, girls wore big, stiff skirts with a wire hoop underneath called a crinoline, and long frilly underpants called pantaloons.

Girls in 1910 wore pale, knee-length cotton dresses with a pastel-colored sash at the waist.

# Body Basics

There's no point in wearing fantastic fashions if your body isn't clean and well cared for. Looking after yourself helps you feel good and makes other people want to be near you!

## Food Facts

To look good on the outside, start on the inside—eat three healthy meals a day to help your body grow and stay strong. Include fresh fruit and vegetables, energy foods such as bread, pasta, and cereal, and foods rich in **protein** such as milk, meat, and fish.

Chocolate, cake, and cookies are fine as a treat every now and then.

## Diet Dangers

Think smart when it comes to food. Avoid eating too much sugary or fatty food, but don't cut out anything completely. Being skinny, hungry, and miserable is not a good look. Plus, you won't have the energy to have fun!

Fruit juices or smoothies keep you going between meals.

## Glug Glug

Water transports all the good stuff from food (called nutrients) around your body and keeps everything working properly. There's no magic amount of water to drink, but the key is to not let yourself get really thirsty. That's your body telling you it needs water urgently!

Most fruit and vegetables contain lots of water.

## Move It!

Exercise gives your body an all-over boost. It makes you fitter and stronger, burns extra sugars and fats, and helps you fight off illness. Do something you enjoy, whether it's a sport, dancing, or going for bike rides with your friends.

## Keep Clean

Wash yourself every morning and evening and change your clothes regularly. Don't neglect your teeth! Bad teeth ruin any look and can make breath smell, too. Brush gently but thoroughly for at least two minutes after breakfast and before bed. Brushing your tongue also keeps your mouth clean.

**Pssst...** Play a favorite song while you're brushing teeth. Then you'll know you've brushed for long enough!

# Super Skin

**N**ot everyone is born with perfect skin. Skin may be naturally oily or dry, or have areas of both. Sensitive skin can break out in a rash when it is hot or as a reaction to skin products or certain foods. Whatever your skin type, it needs looking after!

## Sun Sense

Eating well, drinking water, and exercising help keep skin healthy and soft. Fresh air and sunshine are good for skin too. But sunburn is not! On sunny days, use sunscreen with a sun protection factor (SPF) of 15 or more, and reapply it regularly.

## Scrubbing Up

You don't need to put lots of fancy products on your face. Just wash it well twice a day. Try using a mild, non-perfumed face **cleanser**, as soap may dry out your skin. It's best to avoid wearing makeup as this blocks **pores** and must be removed thoroughly.

Be kind to your skin – stay in the shade when it's really hot, and wear a hat.

**Pssst...** Test new products (even natural ones) on a small area of skin first to check you aren't **allergic** to them.

## Nice and Natural

Natural ingredients such as honey and milk have been used for many years to soften and soothe skin. Try them in the bath by adding about ½ cup (120 mL) each of honey and powdered milk to running water.

Tea, herbs, and fruit peels can make gentle baths or foot soaks. Here's an easy one to try.

**1.** *Cut the toe from a pair of tights to make a bath bag.*

**3.** *Tie the top, put the bag in the bath and run hot water. Let it soak for five minutes, then add cold water until the bath is the right temperature. Get in and relax!*

**2.** *Snip the tops off three teabags of green tea and pour it into the bag. Add a tablespoon (15 mL) of freshly-grated ginger and the grated rind of a lemon.*

**Try adding lavender, replacing lemon peel with orange, or using other herbal teas.**

**Skin Trends**

Fashionable women in eighteenth-century Europe stuck velvet or silk **beauty spots** on their faces.

In the past, people wanted pale skin to show that they were rich enough not to have to work outdoors. One skin-lightening powder from Japan was made of bird droppings!

Mehndi is an Indian style of decorating skin using dye from **henna** plants.

# Lovely Lips

**L**ips are a very noticeable part of your face, so make sure they look their best. Skin on lips is thin and tender, and can easily dry and crack. Treat it with care.

### Cover Up

Using **petroleum jelly** or a medicated lip **balm** is a great way of keeping lips soft. It makes them look nice and shiny, too! In sunny weather, make sure your balm has sun protection (SPF 15 or above).

## Lip Tips

Beware of using lipsticks and lip glosses. They dry your lips and make **chapped** lips look even worse. They can also smudge and end up all over your teeth and clothes! Tinted lip balms look just as good and are much kinder to lips.

## Jazzy Lip Gels

*To make your own tinted, flavored lip balm, put a spoonful of petroleum jelly in a microwavable bowl, melt it in the microwave for about 40 seconds, then stir until it's liquid.*

**Be careful – the bowl may get hot.**

*Mix in a spoonful of strawberry milkshake powder, then pour the mixture into a small clean jar or a plastic lid. When it has set, you'll have your own strawberry lip balm!*

**Make more fun balms using other milkshake flavors, edible cake glitter, food coloring, or a few drops of vanilla extract!**

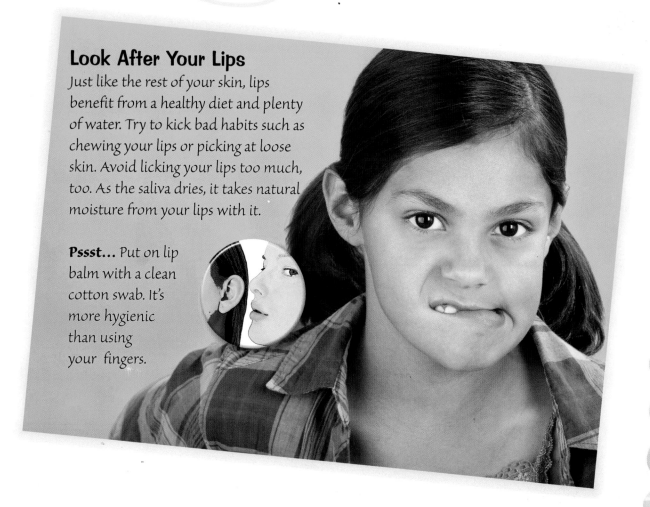

## Look After Your Lips

Just like the rest of your skin, lips benefit from a healthy diet and plenty of water. Try to kick bad habits such as chewing your lips or picking at loose skin. Avoid licking your lips too much, too. As the saliva dries, it takes natural moisture from your lips with it.

**Pssst...** Put on lip balm with a clean cotton swab. It's more hygienic than using your fingers.

# Gorgeous Hair

**H**aving great-looking hair is a two-part process. First, help it grow strong and healthy by eating well, drinking water, and getting enough fresh air, exercise, and sleep. Next, treat it kindly!

## Easy Does It

To avoid breaking and damaging wet hair, pat it dry with a towel, then comb through with a wide-toothed comb. Let your hair dry on its own if possible, as blow-drying blasts away natural moisture and can make it brittle and dull.

Try fun temporary hairstyles using curlers, or **crimp** straight hair by drying it in braids.

## Smart Snips

Have hair trimmed regularly, but don't be tempted by a new cut that needs lots of tricky styling. Ask a hairdresser which low-maintenance looks could suit you. But don't feel you have to go for the cut they suggest.

## Be Creative

Keep your hairdo exciting by using hair clips and headbands, or wear a scarf (see page 23). If your hair is long enough to tie up, try this cute hair bow.

**1.** Brush hair into a ponytail on top of your head and wrap a hair tie around it a couple of times. The last time, leave the hair in a loop, like this.

**2.** Fan out the loop and gently divide it in half.

**3.** Take the end of the ponytail and pull it to the back. Use two bobby pins in an X to pin the end under the ponytail.

**4.** You could add a bit of hair spray to keep your bow neat.

*If you have lots of thick hair, try making a bow from just one section of hair.*

**Pssst...** Swimming pool chemicals can damage hair, so wear a swim cap or make sure you rinse your hair afterwards.

# Historical Hairdos

Ancient Egyptians kept cool by shaving their heads. They wore long, dark wigs for special occasions.

Eighteenth-century women styled their hair over a tall, padded wire frame and added fake hair to make it look even bigger.

In the 1920s, many young women shocked their parents by having short, **bobbed** haircuts.

# Perfect Nails

**N**ails may be small, but they say a lot about you. Dirty, bitten, or ragged nails can ruin a stylish outfit and make you feel self-conscious about your hands, while well-groomed nails project an image of elegance, whatever you're wearing.

Who needs extra accessories when you can show off beautiful nails?

### Be Nice to Nails

Help your nails grow healthily by eating a balanced diet (see pages 6-7). Try not to bite them, and rub in moisturizing cream if the skin around the nails looks dry or flaky. Clean under each nail using cotton swabs.

**Pssst...** Don't forget your toenails! Keep them clean and cut straight across, as shaping sides can lead to **ingrown toenails**.

## Time for a Trim

You may love the idea of long, tapering talons, but shorter, wider nails look chic and are less likely to split or break. Keep them all the same shape and length. Cut straight across with nail scissors, then use an **emery board** to file the edges into a squared-off oval.

Filing in just one direction helps to create a smoother edge.

Don't file too low at the sides or you'll weaken the nail.

## Painting Nails

To apply nail polish neatly, paint steady strokes up each nail. Start in the middle and work to the sides. Let it dry, then add another layer so the polish lasts longer. With strong shades, paint a clear layer first so the color doesn't stain your nails.

Always take off polish with polish remover as soon as it begins to flake. Old, chipped nail polish does not look good!

## Nail Art

Here are some fantastic ideas for noticeable nails. Try them with friends so you can share colors. Then sit and chat while you wait for each layer to dry!

## Dainty Dots

**1.** Paint your nails and let dry.

**2.** Dip the end of a toothpick or straightened bobby pin into a different color and dot it on your nails. Try making patterns or flowers.

**3.** For a professional look, add a layer of clear polish when the dots are dry.

## Show-Stopping Stripes

**1.** Choose two colors that work well together. Paint nails with one color.

**2.** Stick thin strips of masking tape over each nail, then paint with the second color, going across the nails.

**3.** When polish is dry, carefully peel off tape.

**4.** Try diagonal stripes or sprinkle glitter on wet polish for extra dazzle.

# What's in Your Closet?

**N**ow that your body's looking good and feeling great, you can start thinking about what to dress it in! But before you head off on a shopping spree, stop and look at what you already have. You might surprise yourself.

Have a careful look through all your clothes – you're sure to find stuff you've forgotten about!

## Everything Out!

Start by pulling out all your clothes from closets and drawers, then try on everything. Take a good look in the mirror and be ruthless. Clothes that are worn and shabby, or don't look good, fit well, or feel comfortable have to go!

**Pssst...** Don't throw away unwanted things! Bag them up and take them to a thrift store.

# Clothing Basics

Once you've cleaned out your closet, sort everything into tops, pants, skirts, and dresses, then mix and match different items to see what works together. Here are a few tips to help.

**1.** Layering is a great way of getting the most out of clothes and creating different looks. For example, a summer dress becomes a winter outfit with a cardigan and leggings or thick tights underneath.

**2.** Don't wear too many colors at once, and make sure they work well together. Use layers to add splashes of color.

**3.** Go easy on very sparkly or busy clothes! Team just one eye-catching piece with plain items.

**4.** Outfits that are very tight or really baggy look unflattering, so create balance by pairing loose tops with narrow pants, and clingy tops with wider pants.

Get into the habit of hanging up your clothes rather than leaving them in piles on chairs or the floor!

## Be Organized

If you can't see clothes, you won't wear them, so organize! Hang similar items together and don't overstuff drawers or it'll be hard to find things and everything will be wrinkled.

# Let's Shop!

**S**hopping for new clothes can be fun, but sometimes you end up with sore feet, an empty purse and stuff you're not sure you'll ever wear! Here's how to make sure your shopping trip is a success.

## Have a Plan

Think about what you need before you hit the stores. If you've organized your closet, you'll know which gaps to fill. For example, everyone needs a good pair of jeans and basic tops that can be layered for different occasions.

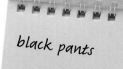

black pants

cardigan that goes with white shirt

denim skirt

Make a list and try to stick to it. Wear or take items that you want to match.

Help to make your shopping spree a success by planning a route, allowing plenty of time, and stopping for regular breaks.

## Money Matters

Be sensible with money and know how much you (or your parents!) can afford to spend. Avoid ridiculously expensive stores, and remember that you can find great bargains in thrift stores. Only splurge on one item if it's something you'll wear a lot, such as a heavy winter coat.

## Try Before You Buy

Everybody has certain styles and colors they prefer, but be brave, too—it doesn't do any harm to try on something different! Put it on then ask yourself, "Does this look good and do I feel happy in it?" Trust your instincts. If in doubt, don't buy it.

## Don't Panic!

Never buy something just because you don't want to go home empty-handed. Treat yourself to a milkshake or a magazine instead and leave shopping for another day. And don't feel you should buy the same thing as your friends. What looks good on them may not be right for you.

Before buying anything, decide whether it will go with the clothes you already have.

**Pssst...** Practice sitting down in clothes before you buy them. If they gape awkwardly or wrinkle instantly, they're never going to look great.

# Funky Fashion

**T**ruly stylish people don't just follow fashion trends. They add personal touches that make clothes look fresh and stand out from the crowd. Try your hand at fashion design with these quick and clever ideas.

## Bling It Up

How about cutting off boring buttons and replacing them with more exciting ones? You could also stitch lace or ribbon to plain **hems** or necklines, or use fabric glue and stick on beads or sequins.

Try stitching layered **felt** shapes and buttons on to jeans or jackets.

**Pssst...** Ask someone who's handy with a sewing machine to help you alter clothes.

## T-shirt Twist

Here's a brilliantly simple way to make a wide T-shirt more fitted and elegant.

**1.** Find a length of ribbon that works well with the T-shirt color. It could be a matching shade or an attractive contrast.

**2.** Using sharp scissors, <u>carefully</u> make two snips about halfway down the front of the T-shirt.

The length of each slit should be about half the width of the ribbon.

**3.** Thread the ribbon through one slit and out of the other. Put on the T-shirt and tie the ribbon to pull the top together.

## Stylish Slashes

Be brave and take a pair of scissors to a plain, stretchy top!

chalk line

**1.** Use chalk to draw a line about 2 in. (5 cm) from the side. Cut up to the line in 1 in. (2 cm) strips.

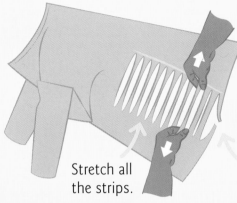

**2.** Open out the cut section and gently stretch each strip so the sides curl over. Cut the bottom strip in half. Rub out the chalk.

Stretch all the strips.

Last strip cut in half.

**3.** Take the top strip and pull it over the second one…

…then take the second strip and pull it over the third in the same way. Take the third strip, pull it over the fourth, and so on.

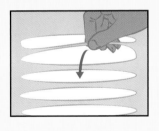
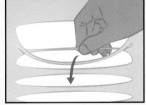
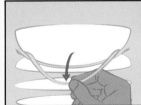

**4.** Pull the two halves of the cut strip through the last loop and knot in the corners.

**5.** Follow steps 1–4 for the other side of the top, then wear it over a T-shirt in a contrasting color. You could also make slashes across the back of a top or down each arm.

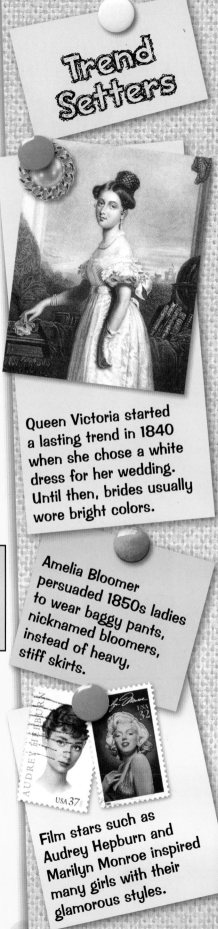

# Accessorize!

**J**ewelry and other accessories liven up outfits and add a personal touch. But remember the golden rule: don't wear too much! Too many accessories look busy and get in the way.

**Pssst...** Look out for another book in this series, ACCESSORIES, for tips on wearing and making all kinds of fabulous accessories.

### Bling Basics

Choose one key jewelry item, such as a chunky necklace on a plain top or silver bangles with black three-quarter length sleeves. Keep other jewelry small and simple. Avoid matching jewelry sets – they look overpowering!

Your accessories can be delicate and dainty (left) or big and bold (right).

### Choose Carefully

Belts, bags, hats, and scarves add splashes of color, but again, choose just one eye-catching piece. A sparkly red belt can turn jeans and a white T-shirt into a chic outfit—but adding lots of red items makes you look as if you raided the dress up box!

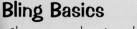

## Shop Smart

There are so many cheap and cheerful accessories in the shops that it's easy to get carried away! Don't forget to look in thrift stores for old or unusual items, swap things with friends or borrow from your mom—asking nicely first, of course!

## Super Scarves

Long scarves are so versatile—as well as going around your neck, they make great ribbons for straw hats, hair ties for ponytails, and even belts for pants. Here are some quick ideas.

*For a neat look, fold a scarf and tie it at the side of your neck, keeping it wide and flat on your forehead.*

*For a more casual look, cross the ends of the scarf on top of your head, twist them once, then tie them at the back of your neck.*

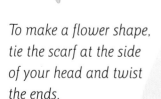

*To make a flower shape, tie the scarf at the side of your head and twist the ends.*

*Hold the end of the twist and coil it tightly. Tuck the end in the twist.*

# Stepping Out

The right shoes make clothes look great, but that doesn't mean you need a new pair for every outfit! Stick to simple styles and a few pairs of shoes will go with most clothes.

## Keep Them Comfy

You may dream of towering heels, but they won't be comfortable and will make you walk awkwardly. Flat shoes, boots, and sandals look just as stylish, and are better for your feet as long as you pick pairs that fit well.

Your feet are still growing, so it's best to have them measured.

Choose plain or dark shades for winter and light, bright patterns for summer.

## Shoe Care

People notice scuffed shoes, so treat them kindly! Store them neatly and wipe or polish them regularly. Remember that worn soles or heels can be replaced.

**Pssst...** Always peel stickers off new shoes before you wear them. Walking around with price tags on your soles is not a good look!

## What's That Whiff?

Sneakers or shoes worn on bare feet can get sweaty. Avoid smells by loosening laces overnight and making sure air can get in and out. Put talcum powder, dryer sheets, or baking soda inside them after you take them off. You could even use a homemade bath bag!

## Fancy Footwear

Give lace-up shoes a personal touch by swapping laces for ribbons or threading on beads. You could also draw bright designs on canvas shoes using **fabric pens**.

Liven up boring sneakers with colorful laces!

# Fun Foot Facts

Until about 1800, shoes weren't shaped differently for left and right feet.

Very long, pointy shoes were fashionable in the fifteenth century. To avoid tripping over the point, people held it up with string and tied the end around their knee!

For many years, people wore wooden outdoor shoes called pattens that fitted over normal shoes and protected them from mud.

# Strike a Pose

**W**hatever you're wearing, it looks so much better if you have great posture. Stand up straight, relax your shoulders, and instantly you'll look more elegant and confident. You'll feel it, too.

### Perfect Photos

When celebrities are photographed, they usually turn their upper body at a slight angle to the camera, point one foot forward, and put their weight on the back foot. Try this yourself. But don't overdo it or you'll end up looking silly!

**Pssst...** To look good in photos, relax and think of something happy, so you smile naturally instead of grinning.

## Sit Up!

Do you spend hours slouched on the sofa or hunched over the computer? Try to keep a straight back when sitting, with your knees at a right angle and your feet flat on the floor. Sitting properly may help you avoid backaches when you're older!

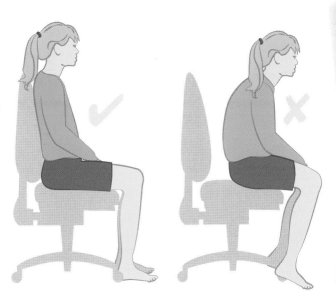

Texting can be terrible for your posture! Keep your shoulders down and your head up.

## Relax

You look better when you feel comfortable, so make sure your clothes fit well and that you're not constantly tugging your skirt down or pushing up shoulder straps. Don't play with your hair and try not to fidget.

## Smooth Moves

No one looks poised and glamorous when they're running for a bus or bursting into class late. Be organized so you can take your time and stay cool. Try dance, sports, or **yoga** classes to get fit, improve posture, and move gracefully.

Heavy bags drag you down and make you hot and bothered. Only carry what you need!

Sports such as gymnastics can help improve your balance, strength, and flexibility.

# Keep Smiling

**W**hen you look in the mirror, it's easy to focus on things you don't like about yourself. Maybe you hate your nose, or think you're too short, or tall, or big, or skinny—everyone has something! Try to concentrate on your good points instead.

**Pssst...** If someone looks good, tell them! It'll make their day to get a compliment And you'll feel good too.

Sometimes features you don't like, such as your hair, height, or shape, may be the envy of your friends!

28

## Think positive

Use your clothes and accessories to show off things you like about your appearance, such as lovely thick hair or dainty hands. Don't bother trying to hide things you can't change. Remember that they are less obvious to other people than they seem to you.

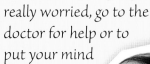

Wearing braces to straighten teeth is so common that people don't think anything of it.

## Keep it Real

So your hair dried all funny or there's a zit on your chin. Try to keep things in perspective and don't obsess over your body. Talk about problems with friends and family. If you're really worried, go to the doctor for help or to put your mind at ease.

## Have Fun!

When you feel happy, you look better, so enjoy pampering yourself and experimenting with fashion, but never take it too seriously. Don't get hung up on trying to look like your favorite celebrity—after all, they have teams of stylists to help them look great!

Remember that real girls don't look like models in glossy magazines.

**BLUSHING** This usually happens when you're stressed or embarrassed. Breathe deeply, relax, and try to ignore it. Boost your confidence by joining a drama group or other club.

**BIRTHMARKS** These harmless patches or spots make you unique! Some can be removed with lasers, but most are best left alone.

**FRECKLES** These mean your skin is fair—so wear plenty of sunscreen on sunny days. Many people think freckles are cute!

# Glossary

**allergic**
Very sensitive to a particular substance, which causes your body to react badly, for example by feeling itchy or getting a rash.

**baking soda**
A white powder, also called sodium bicarbonate. It is often used in cooking, indigestion treatments, mouthwash, and stain removers—it also absorbs strong smells.

**balm**
An ointment used to heal or soothe skin.

**beauty spots**
Another name for dark skin marks called moles. Some people stick or draw beauty spots on their faces. In the eighteenth century, beauty spots were often in the shape of hearts or stars, and were stuck on different places on the face to send coded signals to admirers!

**bobbed**
Hair cut straight around the head, usually at jaw level, often with bangs at the front.

**chapped**
Cracked, rough, or sore. Lips often become chapped in cold weather.

**cleanser**
A gentle lotion or cream for cleaning skin.

**crimp**
To give straight hair lots of waves or kinks.

**emery board**
A cardboard nail file coated in a type of sandpaper. Emery boards are cheaper to buy and gentler on nails than metal files. Throw them away when the scratchy surface starts to wear down.

**fabric pens**
Special pens containing permanent ink that is designed not to fade or wash out of fabric.

**felt**
Fabric made from matted wool. Felt is easy to cut and doesn't fray at the edges. It also comes in lots of bright colors.

**hem**
The edge of a piece of material or clothing that has been turned under and sewn down to make a finished edge.

**henna**
A flowering plant. Henna leaves are dried, ground, and mixed into a paste to dye skin, hair, and nails reddish-brown.

**ingrown toenails**
Toenails that curl and grow into skin at the sides of the toe, making the skin red, swollen, and sore. This may happen if nails are badly cut, broken, or squished into tight shoes.

**petroleum jelly**
A clear or pale yellow ointment that creates a waterproof coating when smeared on lips or skin.

**pores**
Tiny holes in your skin. When pores become clogged with dirt and oil, pimples can form.

**protein**
A substance found in animals and plants that is vital for building cells in your body and keeping bones, muscles, skin, and other body parts strong and healthy.

**yoga**
A type of exercise that uses stretching, balancing, and relaxation techniques to help improve your body's strength and flexibility.

# Smart Sites

**www.fashion-era.com**
Fascinating facts on fashion styles through history, from ancient underwear to this year's top trends, plus tips for designing your own fashions.

**www.scarves.net/how-to-tie-a-scarf**
Step-by-step instructions and helpful videos on scarf-tying.

**www.wikihow.com/Be-Photogenic**
How to look good and feel relaxed when having your photo taken.

**www.superbherbs.net/remedies2.htm**
All about herbs and how to use them to cleanse skin, make hair shine, and maybe even soothe headaches, indigestion, or colds.

**www.helensstyle.com/nail-designs**
Amazing nail polish designs, video tutorials on how they're done, and lots of ideas for creating your own fantastic nail art.

# Index